Promises and Turtle Shells

Dorothy Brenner Francis

Abingdon Press
Nashville

W9-CFJ-342

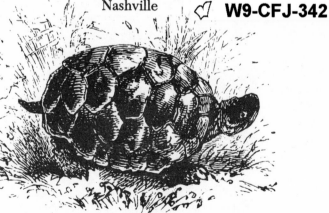

And 49 Other
Object Lessons for Children

Promises and Turtle Shells

Library of Congress Cataloging in Publication Data

FRANCIS, DOROTHY BRENNER
  Promises and turtle shells.
  1. Children's sermons. 2. Object-teaching.
  I. Title.
  BV4315.F643   1984   252'.53   83-21536

ISBN 0-687-34337-2

MANUFACTURED BY THE PARTHENON PRESS AT
NASHVILLE, TENNESSEE, UNITED STATES OF AMERICA

TO
Andrew and Daniel

CONTENTS

ARE YOUR EARS ON?

Prop: *A CB Radio*

You probably all know that some cars are equipped with CB radios. These are radios that let a person in one car talk with a person in another car as they are driving down the highway. Maybe you've listened to people talk over a CB radio, and maybe you've even done a little talking yourself.

When I'm listening to my CB radio, every once in a while I hear someone ask, "Do you have your ears on?" Now that seems like a silly question, doesn't it? People can't take their ears off. But what the CB operators mean is, "Is anyone out there listening?"

There is a lot of difference between having your ears on and actually listening. Have you ever thought about that? Sometimes mothers may think their children don't have

7

their ears on after they've called them to dinner five times and received no response. And it works the other way too. Sometimes kids think their parents don't have their ears on when they try to tell them about what happened that day at school and nobody seems to be interested in listening. You can tell when a parent is just saying, "uh-huh" or "isn't that nice" and when he really has his ears on and is listening to you, can't you?

Children need to have their ears on when they're listening to their parents, and parents need to have their ears on when they listen to their children. Children also need to have their ears on when they're listening to their teachers. Sometimes it's really easy to turn your ears off, isn't it? But you probably regret it later. All of a sudden you realize you don't know what the next day's assignment is. Or maybe you know the teacher is waiting for you to answer a question, but you didn't really hear what the question was. About that time you're sitting there with everyone looking at you, and you really wish you had kept your ears on.

People who want to get the most out of life make careful listening a habit. By listening they can help others, and others can help them. Why don't you make a New Year's resolution to keep your ears on? Make listening a habit.

Sentence Prayer: Our Father, we thank you for our ears and for the ability to use them. Amen.

DRESS FOR SUCCESS

Prop: *A basketball suit*

Look at this costume I'm holding up. If you saw a person wearing this outfit, what would he be? That's right. He'd be a basketball player. Did you ever stop to think how important clothes can be to a person? Now I don't mean that clothes have to be expensive or elaborate to be important. Not at all. Take this basketball suit for example. It's just some colored bits of fabric; but it's appropriate. It's exactly the right thing for a basketball player to wear when he's playing basketball.

Can you imagine a basketball player wearing bib overalls or a suit and a tie? He wouldn't look like a basketball player at all, would he? Once he has on a basketball suit he knows he looks okay, so he can forget about himself and concentrate on his teammates and on the game they're playing.

9

The kind of clothes you wear can be important because they make you feel a certain way. It isn't necessary for them to be expensive, it's only necessary for them to fit the activity you are taking part in. Did you ever stop to think that the clothes you're wearing can determine the way you act?

Probably most of you have certain clothes that you wear to church and Sunday school. And maybe those clothes are just a little bit special. The shoes have a shinier shine. The dress has an extra ruffle or two. The suit has sharp creases in the pants. Now how would you feel if you wore that Sunday outfit on a picnic? You wouldn't feel comfortable at all, would you? And if you didn't feel comfortable you wouldn't act comfortable. You wouldn't feel like playing football or baseball in your Sunday outfit and you probably wouldn't be successful at the game.

What would happen if you wore your everyday jeans with the hole in the knee and the frayed cuffs to Sunday school? You wouldn't feel very comfortable about that either, would you? You might think you would, but when you arrive and see everyone else in their special Sunday clothes you might become so self-conscious over what you are wearing that you can't concentrate on the planned activities.

If you want to be successful in whatever you're going to do, the first thing for you to do may be to dress appropriately for that activity. Once you feel comfortable about how you look, then you can forget about yourself and think about what you are doing and what the others around you are doing. Sometimes forgetting self is one of the important keys to success.

•

Sentence Prayer: Our Father, help us think less of self as we work for good in the world. Amen.

STRETCH YOUR IMAGINATION

Prop: *A lead pencil*

What is this thing I'm holding up here? Right. It's a lead pencil. How many of you own a lead pencil? I suppose all of you have had many pencils in your life, haven't you? They aren't hard to find. They really don't cost too much. You can buy one for just a few cents at the grocery store or the variety store or the drug store.

What do you do with a lead pencil? That's right. You write with it. At least that's what most people think of doing with it. But now I want you to use your imagination. I want you to think of ten other things a person could use a lead pencil for.

(Pause here and accept some ideas from the children. When they run out, supply some of your own.) You might use a lead pencil:

1. to mark your place in a book
2. for a plant stake
3. to dial a phone
4. to advertise a product
5. to dig a hole in the ground
6. to shoot a rubber band

Probably if you really put your mind to it you might be able to think of a hundred things a person could do with a lead pencil besides writing with it.

When I think of all the uses for a pencil, it also makes me think of all the uses for a human life such as yours and mine. We can be anything we want to be. We can be many things. A human being can be a teacher or a minister or a football player or a radio announcer. The list is endless. You can go as far in making such a list as your imagination allows.

When you stop to think about it, a person can go as far in life as he allows his imagination to take him. It's a well-known fact that children are sometimes more imaginative than grownups, so perhaps now is the time for you to practice stretching your own imagination. You can play imagination games with lead pencils or with oranges or with rubber bands. But you can also play imagination games with your own life. What can you imagine yourself to be next week, next year, ten years from now. Put your imagination to work and see where it takes you.

Sentence Prayer: Our Father, we thank you for our imaginations and for your help in using them. Amen.

BALD IS BEAUTIFUL

Prop: *A wig*

You've probably noticed that most of you have lots of hair on your heads. Pretty hair, too. Some is brown and some is red and some is blonde and some is black. But the point is that you all have hair. Now when you look around you, sometimes you'll see people without any hair or maybe without much hair. Have you noticed that? When a person has no hair we say he is bald.

Once I heard a little boy ask his grandfather why he was bald-headed. Now that's not a very polite question to ask, but this grandfather understood that at times children don't really know what's polite and what's not. He looked at his grandson with a twinkle in his eye as he replied.

"Jimmy," he said. "I don't have any hair on my head because my head is perfect."

"It is?" Jimmy's eyes grew a bit wider.

"Sure it is. Whenever God created a perfect head he left it without any hair so everyone could see how perfect it was. But there were so many heads to create that angel helpers sometimes took over that job. Now whenever those angel helpers made a mistake on a head, God stepped in and gave the angel a second chance by letting him create hair to cover up the mistake."

Jimmy thought about that for a while. Then he realized that his grandfather was just teasing him, and they both laughed. But when you think about it, to try to repair a mistake is usually a good idea. Everyone makes mistakes. Do you know anyone who has never made a mistake? I sure don't. Mistakes help us grow and learn. But if you make a mistake and there is something you can do to fix it up, it's a good idea to try to do that. Almost everyone will give you a second chance.

Sometimes if you say the wrong thing to a person you might be able to make things right by apologizing. Sometimes if you make a mess either at home or at school, you can make things right by cleaning it up yourself and not leaving it for someone else to deal with. A good cleanup job can be your second chance.

Whenever you make a mistake, think about a person with a bald head. Or better yet, think about a person with hair. Smile a little if you can, then try to repair your mistake, doing whatever is necessary to make things right again.

Sentence Prayer: Our Father, we thank you for second chances. Amen.

MAKE THIS
MOMENT COUNT

Prop: *A clock* (with a second hand)

Have you ever noticed how important time is at a basketball game? Usually there is a big clock on the scoreboard that counts off the minutes of the game. And on one side of the playing floor there is a timekeeper who keeps track of every second the ball is in play. Time. Time. Is there time to dribble the ball down the court? Is there time to grab that rebound? Is there time for one more play?

I saw a game once that ended with the score tied. In that case the officials granted three more minutes of play to decide which team would be the winner. You should have heard the crowd shout and cheer. All that excitement was over in three minutes!

And at another game I saw the score tied with only two

15

seconds of playing time left. Now what can anyone do with two seconds? But none of the team members had given up hope of winning. People were on their feet cheering. The pep band was playing. Then when the ball went back into play, there was total silence in that gymnasium—two seconds. How would you have felt if you had been the player with the ball? Two seconds, and the outcome of the game depended on what you would do next!

The player threw the ball at the basket and made the winning points for the team. Two seconds. Those two seconds were very important.

Did you ever stop to think that the time in your life is just as important as the time in a basketball game? It is, you know. Now that doesn't mean that you have to keep running and bouncing a ball every second; nor does it mean that someone is going to be on the sidelines cheering for you every minute.

But when you get right down to basic facts you'll realize that time is the only thing you're really sure of. You can wake up every morning with the reasonable hope that you'll have twenty-four hours to spend. Many of those hours will be programmed for you—eating, sleeping, going to school. And there are probably a few more hours that are decided for you. You have chores to do around the house. You have to study. Maybe you must practice on an instrument.

No matter how many things are decided for you concerning your time, you'll still have some left over. And it's up to you how those extra minutes or hours are spent. You can waste them in front of the TV by not choosing your programs carefully. You can waste them with other people if you don't choose your companions carefully. Or you can use your time to good advantage by resting or playing or studying or engaging in some activity that moves you a little closer toward a chosen goal. Time is important. This moment will not come again.

Sentence Prayer: Our Father, we thank you for goals and for the time in which to pursue them. Amen.

THE CLONE

Prop: *Two identical plants*

How many of you know what a clone is? Every time I hear that word I think that someone has mispronounced clown. But not so. Clone is a word we're hearing more and more these days. A clone is an exact reproduction of a group of cells. A plant is a group of cells. A person is a group of cells.

People have known for a long time that they can root a leaf or a stem from certain plants and create another plant that is identical to the first one. But recently certain scientists have been experimenting, and some of them claim that they can take cells from the human body and create an identical human being. How about that! Now I'm not sure I believe it can be done, but it's an idea that's interesting to think about.

Can you imagine someone taking a few cells from your finger and creating another person just like you—identical in every way? Would you like knowing that another person just like you exists? What if this cloning went on until everyone was exactly like everyone else? That wouldn't be much fun, would it? Half of the fun in life comes from the differences we find in people.

But the thing I keep asking myself is, does the world need another person exactly like me? I've got a lot of faults. Sometimes I'm forgetful. Sometimes I'm just plain lazy about doing the chores I'm supposed to do. And I have a hard time with numbers. Sometimes I find that writing thank-you notes is a big bore. Does the world really need a clone of me?

I doubt that cloning will ever become a fad, but one never knows. The very idea of it is enough to make each of us want to improve his act. Ask yourself what the world would be like if everyone was just like you.

Sentence Prayer: Our Father, we thank you for differences. Help each of us to be the best we can. Amen.

THE PEACH BASKET GAME

Prop: *A basketball*

Did you ever wonder where basketball got its start? I can tell you. It started almost a hundred years ago when Dr. James Naismith, a teacher in the Y.M.C.A. college in Springfield, Massachusetts was seeking a game to fill in between the football and the baseball seasons. He is the man who came up with the idea of basketball.

Do you know why it was named basketball? Dr. Naismith wanted some round metal hoops to attach to high backboards, but he could find none. He was determined to try out his idea right at that moment, so he used what he had at hand. He used some old peach baskets, first removing the bottoms then attaching the basket rims to the backboards. And thus Dr. Naismith gave the game of basketball to the world.

Now what do you suppose might have happened if Dr. Naismith had given his idea up when he couldn't find the metal hoops he wanted? We might never have heard of basketball. Sometimes when you put off doing a thing because you don't have exactly what you want, you never get around to doing that thing at all. Perhaps when you find the thing you need your enthusiasm is gone, and you just drop the whole idea.

It's very important in everyday living to use what you have. It's very important to act. It's very important not to make excuses and not to wait for the exact perfect conditions that you feel are really necessary. Make do. Get your show on the road. Get your ideas going while you're still enthusiastic about them.

Remember Dr. Naismith and the peach baskets. If you have a good idea and if you're enthusiastic about it, the time to act is now.

Sentence Prayer: Our Father, we thank you for good ideas and the ability to carry them out. Amen.

ANANSI THE SPIDER

Prop: *A toy spider or a picture of a spider*

In West Africa at sunset children like to listen to tales about Tiger and Anansi the Spider. These tales used to be called Tiger Tales, but Anansi the Spider changed all that.

"Tiger," Anansi said one day, "I wish the stories the children listen to at sunset were called the Anansi Stories. Because you are so strong you have *many* important things named for you—tiger lilies, tiger moths, tiger sharks. But I have nothing named for me."

Tiger thought for a moment. "All right, Anansi. I'll make a deal with you. You catch a snake and bring him to me alive, and I'll name the stories we tell at sunset the Anansi Stories."

All the animals of the forest laughed. They knew that

one weak spider couldn't catch a strong snake—alive. But Anansi had a plan.

"Snake," Anansi said the next time they met, "I do believe you're the longest animal in the jungle."

"Why, of course I am," Snake said, as he stretched himself out to full length.

"My, my," Anansi said. "I do believe you're as long as that bamboo tree over there."

"Cut the tree and bring it here and we'll see," Snake said.

So Anansi cut the bamboo, trimmed the leaves, and laid it beside Snake. "Well, I don't know, Snake. It's hard to tell. Your tail's at the end of the bamboo all right, but when I run to your head, you could pull your tail up and cheat on me."

"Then tie my tail to the end of the bamboo," Snake suggested. "I'll prove that I'm the longest animal in the jungle."

So Anansi tied Snake's tail to the end of the bamboo. By now all the animals of the jungle had come to watch.

"Stretch, Snake," they called. "You've got six inches to go in order to reach the other end of the bamboo."

Snake stretched and stretched and at last he said to Anansi, "Tie my middle to the bamboo so I won't keep slipping back. I *know* I'm the longest animal in the jungle."

So Anansi tied Snake's middle to the bamboo. "Now, Snake, why not take it easy?" Anansi asked. "Rest a minute. Then close your eyes and stretch as hard as you can. I think you can bring your head right to the end of the bamboo."

So Snake rested. Then he closed his eyes and stretched. While Snake's eyes were closed Anansi pulled a grape-vine from his pocket and tied Snake's head to the end of the bamboo. All the creatures of the forest helped Anansi carry Snake to Tiger.

Tiger was surprised that one weak spider could capture one strong snake—alive. He set Snake free, then he turned to Anansi. "From now on the stories we tell at sundown will be called the Anansi Stories."

And to this day that's what the stories are called—the Anansi Stories. Anansi was a pretty smart spider, wasn't he? He knew what he wanted, and he thought until he found a way to get it. Sometimes we all feel discouraged. Sometimes we think we can't succeed. We think that other people have all the goodies and we have nothing. If you ever start thinking that way you might want to stop and remember the story of Anansi and Snake. There's usually a way to succeed if you'll just try hard enough to find it.

Sentence Prayer: Our Father, thank you for our minds and for your help in using them. Amen.

AGNES ALLEN'S LAW

Prop: *A ring that's too small for a finger*

My grandmother had a friend named Agnes Allen. Now this may not seem very important to you, but Agnes Allen was important in my life because she was always saying wise things. I don't know how she got so smart, but she was always saying things that almost became laws at our house.

Now one of the smart things that Agnes Allen said was, and I quote: "Almost anything is easier to get into than out of." At our house that became known as Agnes Allen's law. Think about it. Look at this ring and look at my finger. If I'm not careful my finger can get stuck, can't it?

Once I saw a picture of a boy who had put his finger into a piece of pipe that he found sticking up from the ground. You guessed it. He couldn't get his finger out. His parents couldn't free the finger, so they called the fire department. The firemen managed to get the boy's finger out of the pipe. Now there was a classic example of Agnes Allen's law at work. That pipe was easier to get into than out of. The boy could have avoided a lot of embarrassment if he had just asked himself how he was going to get his finger out of the pipe, if there was any chance that he might get stuck.

Pipes aren't the only things we can get stuck in. We can get stuck in situations too. One boy I knew told his teacher that his mother would be glad to drive a group of classmates to the aquarium after school the following Tuesday. He chose six friends to go along. When he told his mother she said, "But Bill, next Tuesday I have to be out of town on business." He was into something, wasn't he?

What to do? Agnes Allen's law was really working wasn't it? It had been easy to get into this situation, but now it was going to be hard to get out of it. Bill had made a promise that he couldn't keep and Agnes Allen's law was really letting him have it. There wasn't much he could do but beg off and ease out of his promise. It wasn't easy. He felt very sorry and very embarrassed.

We all run up against Agnes Allen's law now and then. We get ourselves into things that are very hard to get out of. Many times this happens when we talk when we should listen. Try to look ahead at what might come next. Ask yourself if you're about to get into something that's going to be hard to get out of.

Sentence Prayer: Our Father, help us to look ahead and be prepared. Amen.

THOUGHTS
ABOUT FRIENDS

Prop: *A friendship ring*

One day I was visiting at a home where there was a girl about the age of you children. That particular day she was rather unhappy, and she was telling her troubles to her mother. It seems that her best friend, Mary, whose friendship ring she wore every day, had gone off to play with someone else and left her alone. Her friend Sally had whispered about her in arithmetic class the day before, and her friend Julie had teased her about being late for school. Yes, this girl had a long list of complaints about her friends, and I'm sure some of them were valid. I was interested in hearing what her mother would say to her. When I heard I had to chuckle to myself.

Her mother said, "What you say is probably true, Lisa,

but just remember—God never gives you more friends than you can stand."

How true. God never gives any of us more friends than we can stand because he has given us the ability to forgive. We all make mistakes. We all do things we know we probably shouldn't do. Sometimes these things hurt our friends' feelings; and sometimes our friends hurt our feelings. But we can still keep our friendships brightly shining if we use our capacity to forgive.

If you really value your friendship with another person, then you'll be willing to give that person room for a few mistakes, won't you? And he'll do the same for you.

On those days when your friends all seem to have deserted you, be patient. They'll be back. And you'll greet them with a smile when they return. God never gives us more friends than we can stand.

Sentence Prayer: Our Father, we thank you for the ability to forgive and to be forgiven. Amen.

THAT SPECIAL FREEDOM

Prop: *A do-it-yourself kit*

This era we're living in may be called the space age, but it might also be called the age of the do-it-yourself kit. How many of you have made something from a kit? Maybe you've built a model car or a model airplane or a picture to hang on the wall. Kits are a lot of fun to work with. They can be the basis of a hobby that will give you hours of pleasure all through life.

Now you may not have thought of this, but each of us works with a very important do-it-yourself kit every day. Do you know what that kit is? It's your life. Did you ever think of that? You're building your own life day by day and your do-it-yourself kit might be called your free will or your freedom of choice.

By using freedom of choice you make decisions that

determine how your life will turn out. Of course, you may get help from others, from teachers and parents and friends. But that's the same way it is with any kit, isn't it? Sometimes you may need to call on Mom or Dad or a brother or a sister for a helping hand. But for the most part you do it yourself.

In building a model car you have to be careful to follow the rules, don't you? It's the same thing in building your life. There are rules to follow. You have the Ten Commandments for starters. And every family has some rules of its own. Your school has more rules. You may get tired of rules and directions sometimes, but they are there to help you.

It's not easy to build a model plane or a model car, and it's not easy to build a life either. But in all cases it will help if you do your best to follow the rules.

Sentence Prayer: Our Father, we thank you for the gift of free will. Help us to use it wisely. Amen.

USE YOUR OWN DIME

Prop: *A dime*

How many of you know what a pay telephone is? You probably don't have one in your home. You can just pick up your telephone receiver and dial the number you want without paying, can't you? But sometimes you'll see telephones that won't work unless you put some money in a pay slot. In some places it's only a dime.

How many of you have been in an airport or a hospital or some other public building where there was a row of pay telephones for people to use? What did you do when you saw those telephones?

Sometimes you'll see a child walk along the row of telephones. He'll poke his finger in a tiny slot labeled "coin return" above it. And sometimes he'll be lucky and pull out a nickel or a dime or a quarter. How can that happen?

If someone dials a number and nobody answers, the telephone operator will return the caller's money. You hear it clink inside the telephone box as it falls into the coin return slot. But sometimes if the caller is in a hurry he may forget to collect his coin. Some children make it a habit to check out the slots on all pay telephones when they have a chance. Have you ever done this? Have you ever found a coin? Usually you don't find anything.

I've seen grown-ups look in the coin return slot when they didn't have the right change for the pay phone. But usually they found nothing to help them. They had to use their own money. And that's the way it is in life. You'll have better luck at everything you do if you just plan to use your own dime and not depend on getting any freebies.

You know how it goes. Have you ever gone to school without a pencil? Then what do you do? You try to borrow from a friend. Sometimes he has an extra one, and sometimes he doesn't. Or maybe you forgot your lunch or your lunch money. You might be lucky and find a friend to help you out of your trouble. Or you might have to go hungry. The smart thing to do is to think ahead, to plan for your own needs so you won't have to depend on luck or on others to get you through the day.

Before you leave home in the mornings maybe you'll want to stop for a second and think of a pay telephone. Remember, smart people plan to use their own dimes.

Sentence Prayer: Our Father, we thank you for the strength to help ourselves as well as others. Amen.

THE LAST WORD

Prop: *Picture of a Greek wood nymph*

How many of you have brothers or sisters at home? Do you ever get angry at your brothers or sisters or at your friends? Do you argue with them? Most of us have done that at some time or other in the past. Somehow we seem to find it satisfying to have the last word. "You can't." "Yes I can." "No you can't." "Yes I can too."

Have you heard arguments go on like that? Sometimes a person just won't give up until he can have the last word. Now I can remember a time many years ago when I always wanted to have the last word. Sometimes I would argue until my brothers and sisters gave up and let me have the last word. Then one day my grandmother told me the story of Echo.

How many of you know what an echo is? Sure you

33

know. If you shout into a cave or a mountain valley you'll hear the echo of your own voice, won't you? Your words will come back to you.

According to Greek mythology there was once a mountain nymph named Echo. Now Echo was a lovely girl, but she had one fault: she talked all the time. Whenever there was silence, she filled it with her voice. One day Zeus was talking to some nymphs when the goddess Hera appeared. Now Hera really disliked for Zeus to talk to the nymphs, and Echo knew this. So to distract Hera, Echo began talking to Hera.

Hera was so busy listening to Echo get in the last word that the other nymphs had a chance to run hide. In a few moments Hera realized that Echo had tricked her and she was very angry.

"You will be punished," Hera said. "Echo, from now on you will always have the last word."

Now Echo thought that sounded like a light punishment until she realized the last word was *all* she could have. She could never have the first word. One day she met a handsome hunter and fell in love, but she couldn't tell him she loved him because she couldn't have the first word. She followed him over the mountainside, but she couldn't speak to him. One day he heard her, but before he turned to see who was following him Echo hid.

"Who is there?" he called.

"There?" she replied.

"Are you keeping away from me?" he called.

"Away from me," she answered.

And as if her words were a command, the hunter left her, and she couldn't say the first word to call him back.

Now that is a sad story isn't it? I always think about it when I'm tempted to try to have the last word in an argument. I stop and ask myself, "What if the last word is all you can have?" And usually when I think of that, I stop the argument. Wouldn't you?

Sentence Prayer: Our Father, we thank thee for our voices. Teach us to use them wisely. Amen.

STORMY WEATHER

Prop: *A lightning rod*

When you're riding in the country do you ever notice the rods on top of some farm buildings? Many times barns will have several metal rods set on the ridge of the roof. If you've noticed those rods you may have wondered what they are. Those are lightning rods.

A lightning rod is placed on a building for a reason. It is installed to divert lightning away from the building. In stormy weather the farmer hopes that if lightning strikes, it will strike the lightning rod, which will redirect the current of electricity and save his barn from destruction.

Lightning rods are very useful things. Did you ever stop to think that people could serve as lightning rods when there's a storm within a family? Maybe your family is always peaceful and quiet. Some families may be that way, but now and then families have periods of storm within the walls of the home.

Maybe your older brother comes home angry because he didn't rate a place on the ball team. Or maybe your sister comes home angry because she wasn't elected cheerleader. They might feel so bad about what's happened at school that they take their feelings out on the family. Maybe they sulk at the table, and your father is tired of table sulkers and sends them to their rooms.

So perhaps when you go to your room after the meal they say something mean that really makes you want to fight. If this happens—stop.

Remember the lightning rod on the barn. You can pretend your brother or your sister's words are lightning and you can choose what you'll do next. You can flash lightning words back at them and make the storm worse for everyone. Or you can pretend you're a lightning rod and absorb their words, say something pleasant, and let them know you understand how they feel.

If you choose the second way of action you will be diverting the harmful effects of the storm away from the family and leading it harmlessly away from your home. Think about this the next time a storm threatens your family. Ask yourself if there is any way you can serve as a lightning rod and help guide the family to the calm that usually follows every storm.

Sentence Prayer: Our Father, help us to be peacemakers. Amen.

TIME FOR A CHANGE

Prop: *A baby doll*

How many of you have little brothers or sisters? A lot of you do, don't you? And how many of you remember when that brother or sister was born? Some of you can remember, but maybe some of you were too young to really remember when the new baby arrived.

I know a girl who was about four when her little brother was born. Now in some ways she was glad, but in other ways she was a little bit worried. She wondered if her parents would still have any time for her or would that new baby take up all of their time. Would she and Mother still have time to play together? Would Daddy still have time to read her stories? She was really pretty worried about the whole thing.

And then the baby brother arrived. Sure enough, sometimes her mother was busy mixing formula and giving the baby a bath, and sometimes Daddy was busy putting clothes in the washer or rocking the baby to sleep. After a while the girl began to feel left out of things. That baby wasn't as much fun as everyone had said it was going to be.

It was several days before the girl began to notice that her parents were talking about taking the baby back. First she heard her mother say it. "Dear," Mother said to Father, "I think we're going to have to change the baby."

"I guess you're right," Father replied. "I'll do it."

The girl held her breath. Where would Daddy go to change the baby? What would he change it for? A dog maybe? Or a kitten? She thought a dog or a kitten would be fun, but suddenly she knew she would miss the baby. It really was snugly and tiny, and sometimes it smiled just at her. She didn't want her parents to change it. Not at all. She began to cry. Then she finally explained how she felt.

"I don't want you to change the baby," she said. "I want to keep it."

Mother looked at her, then she smiled and said, "We may give the baby a clean diaper now and then, but if you've decided you really want to keep him, we won't change him."

The girl felt much better as she ran to play. That's how many of us are about things. We have a thing and maybe we think we don't like it, but if something happens to make us think we're going to lose it, then it becomes very important to us. We see good things about it that we never saw before.

Whenever you think you're really fed up with someone, stop and think what your life would be like without that other person. You'll probably feel just like the girl who didn't want her folks to change the baby. Even when we don't get the attention we want, it's always good to have nice people around.

Sentence Prayer: Our Father, help us to see the good in other people. Amen.

LETTERS TO NOAH

Prop: *A picture of animals or of an ark*

Y ou've all heard the story of Noah and his ark and about how he chose two animals of each species to be his traveling companions during the great flood that destroyed the land. Have you ever wondered just how Noah decided which animals to take along with him? Surely there must have been many elephants and many goats and many mice on the earth. Surely old Noah had to make some decisions. Just *who* was to go along? That must have been a tough decision.

A poet has created some rhymes that she felt might have come to Noah in application letters before the flood. Surely every animal wanted to go. Surely many of them applied for a position aboard the ark.

Here is what some of the letters might have said:

To: **Noah**
From: **Mouse**
  I'll represent your passengers
  And guarantee they'll never grouse
  About your rules if you'll make me
  The honored Squeaker of the House.

To: **Noah**
From: **Goat**
  I'm a fresh goat from Nantucket
  Who'll ask all your friends to pot-luck it.
  When ark food gets dull
  The ones who have pull
  Can drink my fresh milk from a bucket.

To: **Noah**
From: **Skunk**
  If you get lost
  Just sail by your nose
  I'll help you tell
  Which way the wind blows.

Now the world has no record of whether or not those letters were authentic or what results they generated. But they bear thinking about. Those letters seem to indicate that the people who get chosen for key positions are the people who have something to offer.

Every day each of us is developing new skills and storing worthwhile knowledge. We're all learning how to make ourselves useful to others, aren't we? As you continue to grow and develop, ask yourself what you can do for someone else. Then do it.

Sentence Prayer: Our Father, help us to develop the best there is in us and to use that best to help others. Amen.

WHAT A HABIT!

Prop: *Mother's Day card*

Many children honor their mothers on the second Sunday in May. There are many ways you can honor your mother. You can make her a gift. You can make her a special card and maybe include a poem that you wrote. Or maybe you can make breakfast or lunch for her.

One of the things a mother might like best would be the gift of a promise. A promise gift should not be made lightly. Once when I was young, I promised my mother to keep my room clean for a whole year. Believe me that was a long year! Don't promise more than you can deliver.

A friend of mine promised his mother that he would break one bad habit as a gift to her. And he let her choose the habit. If you did this, what habit do you think your mother would choose?

Maybe she'll ask you to break the habit of a messy room or to quit eating between meals. She may even ask you to give up junk food or to stop overeating and lose ten pounds. Do you bite your nails? She might ask you to stop that habit.

Whatever habit you decide to try to break for your mother you're going to have to really think about it. Habits are formed over a long period of time and it usually takes about as long to break the habit as it took to form it, if not longer.

One way to approach breaking a habit is to think about what you're going to do instead. If you bite your nails and really want to stop, ask yourself what you're going to do instead. Maybe you'll decide that every time you think about biting your nails you'll sit on your hands instead. That might work. Or you might just think of something more worthwhile to keep those hands busy. You could start to paint a picture and paint a bit whenever you feel like nail-biting.

Think about this and mabe you'll want to ask your mother what habit she would like to see you break. A gift of yourself will mean much more than a gift from the store.

Sentence Prayer: Our Father, we thank you for our mothers. Help us in our desire to please them. Amen.

THE PEOPLE OF
TAO CHOU

Prop: *A scroll*

Years ago the emperor of China sent a governor named
Yang Ch'eng to the province of Tao Chou. Now the
people of Tao Chou were dwarfs, and they were unhappy.
They weren't unhappy because they were dwarfs, but
their tears fell like rain because each year at the time of
melon harvest many of them were sent to the emperor's
court to be slaves. The emperor considered them a
natural dwarf-slave product from the land of Tao Chou.

When Yang Ch'eng arrived the people looked to him
for help. "Honorable one, please help us save our
families," a spokesman begged. "My people do not wish
to be a part of the offering of natural products from the
land of Tao Chou. And that is what the emperor calls
us—a natural product of dwarf slaves."

Yang Ch'eng said, "Never before have I heard of a natural product that separates people from families they love. I will try to help." So he wrote a message to the emperor on a scroll saying that the people of Tao Chou no longer wished to serve as slaves at his court. A messenger carried the scroll to the emperor.

Weeks later cherry blossoms were falling when the messenger returned with the dust of a thousand miles upon his cloak. The emperor replied on a scroll. "I command that you send the usual offering of Tao Chou's natural product—dwarf slaves."

The dwarfs wailed like peacocks crying at the dawn. The spokesman once again asked of Yang Ch'eng, "Protect our families, wise one. Plead with the emperor again."

So Yang Ch'eng sent another scroll to the emperor. "In offering products for the esteemed emperor I must offer only what is here. I must not offer what is not here. I cannot offer you what I do not possess. In the land of Tao Chou I only find dwarfish *people*. I find no dwarfish slaves. Thus I am unable to send slaves to your court."

This time the emperor's reply pleased the people. He wrote: "Your concern for the *people* of Tao Chou has touched my heart. The yearly tribute of slaves is annulled. May your *people* live in joy."

Now you may wonder what this tale from China has to do with you, but think about it carefully. Has anyone ever called you a "dummy" or some name you didn't like? That happens to almost everyone at some time. The best way to deal with a name-caller is to show him what you really are. In a quiet way let that name-caller know what you are. When you have the wisdom and the courage to stand up for what you are, the world will listen. Remember the people of Tao Chou. The emperor called them slaves.

They called themselves people. What do you call yourself? You write your own label, so make it a good one.

Sentence Prayer: Our Father, we thank you for the freedom to be what we want to be. Amen.

CELEBRATE WITH JOY

Prop: *Picture of an elephant*

Each year in the city of Surin, Thailand in southeastern Asia there is a celebration honoring the elephant. That may seem unusual to you, but people in Thailand respect and honor the elephant because it has helped them for centuries. In ancient times elephants carried soldiers and kings into war. In modern times the elephants work for people. They push logs to the river and help build buildings. It is for these reasons that people look forward to the Surin festival with such great pleasure and expectation.

On this day elephants are costumed in bright colors for a parade. After the parade there is an elephant rodeo. And after that there is a tug of war—one hundred men on one end of a rope and one elephant on the other end. And guess who usually wins—the elephant.

Now an elephant festival is really rather unusual, but when you think about it all nations and states and cities hold festivals to celebrate the things they are proud of. For example, Pasadena, California is proud of its roses, and each year it holds a famous rose parade. In Pella, Iowa, there is a tulip festival each year. The citizens of Pella, who at one time came from Holland, dress in their native costumes and scrub down the city streets while visitors view the lovely tulip displays.

Festivals can come even closer to home than Thailand or California or Iowa. Your family holds festivals. You may call them parties or celebrations, but they are types of festivals. And why? Christmas. Thanksgiving. New Year's Day. There's a long list. But what else? Maybe you've forgotten one of the most important celebrations.

How about your birthday? Doesn't your family usually do something special to celebrate your birthday? Remember what we said. People hold festivals and celebrations to honor what they are proud of. Your family is proud of you. Never forget that.

Sometimes when you have to make a decision about some action you're about to take you might want to think about your family. Would they be proud of what you're about to do? Sometimes that thought can help you make your decision. Never forget that your family is proud of you.

Sentence Prayer: Our Father, we thank you for our families. Amen.

DO NOT ENTER

Prop: *Replica of a* **Wrong Way–Do Not Enter** *highway sign*

How many of you have seen a sign like this one as you've ridden along the highway? (Hold up and read the sign.) I know that you don't drive, but have you ever seen either of your parents enter a street that was marked with these words? No, I'd guess you haven't, because your parents know that an accident would likely result. Signs like this usually mark streets or highways where the traffic will be coming toward you if you enter. If you went into such a place, you would be in the path of oncoming cars and this would be a very dangerous situation.

Sometimes children tell me that they get tired of hearing grown-ups say "don't do this" and "don't do that." I can understand that. Sometimes it's hard to accept restrictions on our activities. We want to do what we want to do. We don't like to hear the don'ts of life. If you ever feel this way, just remember this highway sign: **Wrong Way–Do Not Enter.**

When somebody gives you a *don't* to live by, they're probably offering it for good reason. They know the danger lurking ahead, a danger that you cannot see. The person who is spouting the don'ts is really acting in your behalf and trying to protect you from a crash.

When you were little someone probably said, "Don't touch the stove." Maybe you went ahead and touched it anyway. If you did you learned it was hot. You could have saved yourself a burned finger by listening to the warning. As we grow older and grow in wisdom we learn to listen to those who can see beyond what we can see. Listen to that person and prevent a crash.

Sentence Prayer: Our Father, we thank you for those with more experience than we have who can show us the way. Amen.

WONDER TIME

Prop: A *calendar showing the summer vacation months*

"What can I do now, Mom?"
"I'm tired of just sitting around, Dad."
Often when summertime arrives parents hear these familiar complaints. I can sympathize with their feelings although I have to think back many years in order to remember when I felt wrapped in a cocoon of nothing to do. But believe it or not having nothing to do can be an advantage. It gives a person time to wonder. Do you ever just sit and wonder about things?

In Florida there is a man named Mel Fisher who wondered about a treasure on the bottom of the sea. He knew that for over two hundred years Spain sent treasure galleons, which are ships, between Madrid and the New World. He knew that many of these galleons sank in the seas near the Florida coast. Where had those galleons gone down? Mel Fisher wondered. He knew how to dive for treasure, but he didn't know where to dive.

Now there was another man in Florida who also was interested in old Spain. His name was Eugene Lyon. Eugene Lyon knew how to speak and read ancient Spanish, but he didn't know how to swim and dive. The sea fascinated him, but he didn't know how to deal with it.

One day Mr. Fisher and Dr. Lyon met, and they realized that each one had knowledge or ability that the other needed so they began working together. Dr. Lyon, being a scholar, worked in the archives (a kind of library) of the Indies in Seville, Spain. He read ancient documents and learned where the treasure ship Atocha sank. He sent this information to Mel Fisher.

After lots of hard work Mel Fisher and his divers found the remains of the Atocha treasure galleon. Thanks to their working together the world now has many beautiful and valuable artifacts from ancient Spain. You may have seen some of this treasure; there have been several TV programs featuring Mr. Fisher and Dr. Lyon.

Are you perhaps wondering where these two men with such vastly different talents met? Remember, they were strangers at first. I'll tell you. They met in a Methodist Sunday school class. Does that make you wonder more? Does it make you look at the person next to you and wonder what talent he has that might go well with a talent you have? We all have talents, you know. And that's another thing to wonder about, isn't it? This summer when you feel wrapped up in the cocoon of nothing to do, why not just relax and take time to wonder.

Sentence Prayer: Our Father, we thank you for giving us time to wonder and marvels to wonder about. Amen.

THE OLD BARN

Prop: *A picture of an old barn*

How many of you like to draw? Almost everyone has had some experience at drawing. Some people like drawing so much that they make a serious study of it, and they are called artists.

Since artists like to draw, sometimes they pack their easel and brushes and go into the country in search of something special to paint or to sketch. Do you know what they often choose as a model? Who has an idea? (Let the children talk about this for a moment or so.)

When you look at a collection of paintings many times you'll find a picture of an old barn. Artists seem to love old barns. The more run-down and neglected the barn is, the more it seems to appeal to them. For a long time I wondered about this.

As I drove along the countryside I saw many things: new houses, cows, horses, goats, new barns. I wondered why artists find old barns so attractive. Finally I asked an artist, and do you know what he said?

"I'm always hunting old barns because they're so interesting," the artist said. "Look at the old stone in the foundation of that barn. Why, it may have been standing there during Civil War times. Look at the patina on that gray weathered wood. I can see traces of red paint here and there. At one time someone kept the barn painted and in use. And see those bales of hay blocking that far window? The barn is still useful even though it looks very worn on the outside."

As the artist talked, I began to see some of the special things he saw about that old barn. And as I drove off I began to think that people are a lot like barns. The older they get the more interesting they become. Of course there aren't many around that can tell you about the Civil War, but there are lots of people around who can tell you really interesting and fascinating things that happened long before you were born.

Why not find some older people, and talk with them? Ask them what people used to do when they were your age. Ask about school or games or hobbies of that time. Older people are usually glad to share interesting things about their lives with you.

Remember the artist painting the old barn. Maybe you could give him a tip. Old people are more interesting than old barns because they can talk and share their lives with you.

Sentence Prayer: Our Father, we thank you that life is a mixture of old and new and that we can learn from each other. Amen.

YOUR CONSTANT COMPANION

Prop: *A mirror*

How many of you have ever had a friend move away, a friend that you liked very much? Many of us have had this happen. We always feel sad when someone we like leaves us, but in this day and age when many families are on the move, we frequently find that people who we really like will be leaving us. Maybe they will return some day. Maybe you can keep in touch with them through letters or telephone calls. But for the most part they will be sharing a very small part of your life in the future.

But as you go through life you will find that there is one person who will be with you always. This person isn't going to leave you. This person couldn't leave you if he wanted to. Do you know who this person is?

I'll show you. (Hold up the mirror and let each child see

his own reflection.) You are the only person in the world you will never lose. Think about that. It's really rather awesome. You're going to have to live with yourself for the rest of your life. Wow!

Since that is the case, it just makes sense to make yourself easy to live with, doesn't it? You wouldn't choose a companion who was constantly grouchy or a companion who was always late or a companion who didn't do his fair share of the work involved in living. Those are just a few of the things that make a person hard to live with.

So now while you're young its time to think a lot about making yourself easy to live with. Remember you're not doing it entirely for the benefit of others. If you get to thinking that way, just take a minute to look in the mirror. There you will see the person you're going to be living with for the rest of your life.

Sentence Prayer: Our Father, thank you for the ability to make ourselves better people. Amen.

TRAVELING WITH CRUISE CONTROL

Prop: *A toy car*

It's always exciting when your family buys a new car isn't it? It probably doesn't happen too often. It's not a weekly thing like buying groceries or a monthly thing like paying the bills. But buying a new car does happen now and then. When your parents are shopping for a new car they'll probably try out lots of models before they make up their minds. They may even let you have a choice as to color or style. And they might take you with them to ride in the new cars they try out.

I tried a new car that had a device called a cruise control. Do you know what that is? A cruise control is a device that keeps your car traveling at the speed you choose even after you take your foot from the accelerator.

Most people only use the cruise control on their cars

when they are out on the highway. If the speed limit is fifty-five miles per hour, they set the cruise control at fifty-five miles per hour. This way they don't have to worry about breaking the speed limit.

Setting the cruise control at the speed limit can be interesting. You'll notice that you pass some cars that are going much slower than you are. Then you'll notice that lots of cars will pass you, even though you are traveling at the maximum speed that the law allows. You wonder how those speeders get by with it; and sometimes they don't. But it doesn't do any good to be concerned about the slow driver or the fast driver. The driver to be concerned about is the driver of your car.

And this is the way it is in life too. You may have an assignment to do at school. Maybe it's arithmetic and maybe you're not too speedy with numbers. As you work you'll notice that some students are working slower than you are. And of course you'll notice that some students are finishing long before you do. You'll be happier if you don't pay too much attention to the fast students or to the slow students. The best thing to do is to set your cruise control at a speed that works for you. You want to work fast enough to get finished within the time limit, but you don't want to work so fast that you'll make mistakes.

Everyone has a speed that's best for him no matter what he is doing. So if you get discouraged at school, or if you start to thinking you're a lot better than some of the others, just remember the car with its cruise control. Don't pay too much attention to the speed at which others are traveling. Just set your own cruise control and work in a way that's best for you.

Sentence Prayer: Our Father, help us to learn to work in a way that's best for us. Amen.

SEASHELLS BY THE SEASHORE

Prop: *Some seashells*

Have you ever enjoyed a vacation near the ocean? What did you want to do when you saw the beach and the ocean? I'm sure you were impressed with the size of it. Maybe you were even a little bit afraid of the way the waves roared toward you.

I'm guessing that as you walked along the beach you noticed the shells washed up by the tide. And you wanted to pick some of them up to take home, right? Had you brought anything to put them in? Maybe you carried some in your hands. Then, you may have filled your pockets? Maybe you took off your shoes and filled them with shells.

After your day at the beach somebody probably asked you what you planned to do with all those shells. I asked some young friends that one time.

"I'm going to make a necklace," one girl said.

"Sure," her sister said. "I'm going to do that too."

I went on about my business, not paying much attention to the shell jewelers until they approached me with their finished products. The older girl had a beautiful necklace made entirely from blue shells. And she was really pleased with it until she saw the necklace her sister had made using a variety of shells. There were pink shells, white shells, orange shells, brown shells. Almost every color a person could imagine was used in her necklace.

The older girl cut her necklace apart, went back to the beach and found more shells. Then she made herself a necklace like her sister's, using all kinds and colors of shells.

As I watched the girls work I thought how much like people those shells were. The all-of-a-kind necklace was beautiful, just as a group of all-of-a-kind people are beautiful. But the mixture of shells was infinitely more interesting, just as a mixture of people is more interesting. Every person has his own special charm to add to a group. In many ways we are all alike, but the ways in which we are different gives life its spice and variety.

Sentence Prayer: Our Father, give us the wisdom to see the charm every person has to offer. Amen.

THE ALPHABET GAME

Prop: *The letter Q*

I was riding along the highway one day listening to the conversation taking place in the back seat among some children.

"Let's play the alphabet game," Bill said.

"Don't want to," Susie said.

"Why not?" Bill asked. "I think it's fun."

"I don't," Susie insisted. "I always get stuck on the letter *Q*."

"But that's what makes the alphabet game so much fun," Bill insisted. "*Q* is a really special letter and it's fun to try to find it."

The conversation reminded me of my own childhood when I had played the alphabet game as we traveled across the country on our summer vacation. Back in those days about the only place you could find a letter Q was on those green and white Quaker State motor oil signs. So the minute a person passed the letter P he started watching for gasoline stations to see if they carried Quaker State motor oil. If you were out in a rural area when you reached the letter Q you could be stalled for quite some time. Every other contestant could catch up with you. And the one who spotted the first letter Q had dibs on it, meaning "rights, claim" and the rest of the players had to find another one.

Yes, the letter Q was quite special in that game. Sometimes I like to compare certain people to the letter Q. Certain people are very special, aren't they? What kind of people do you think are special? I've made my own list and I'll share it with you.

People who always have a smile for you
People who always have a pleasant word to say
People you can depend on to tell the truth
People who have time to listen
People who have time to help
People who take time to care

My list could go on and on, but I'm not going to let it. I want you to make your own list. Just make a list in your mind and maybe you'll want to write it down later. Just think of the kind of people you think are very special Q people. And while you're thinking, you might sort of plan to try to be a Q person yourself.

Sentence Prayer: Father, we thank you for helping us to be special people. Amen.

FACES ON A MOUNTAIN

Prop: *A picture of Mt. Rushmore*

Now if I told you there are three hundred billion stars in the universe, chances are you'd believe me, wouldn't you? After all, you can't really count them to be sure, so you'd probably believe me. But if I tell you a bench has wet paint, my guess is that you're going to test it for yourself. You probably won't be satisfied until you've touched a finger to the surface of that bench to see if the paint is really wet. People are like that.

In South Dakota in an area called the Black Hills there is a carving that is the result of one man's big dream. His name was Gutzon Borglum, and he made a habit of dreaming *big*. And he made his dreams come true. In the Black Hills he carved a gigantic memorial to four presidents: George Washington, Thomas Jefferson,

Theodore Roosevelt, and Abraham Lincoln. Borglum was different from most people. He couldn't believe completely in his big dream until he could touch it just as if it were a commonplace thing like wet paint.

So he went to work. At first there was only a narrow logging trail back to that granite mountain, but Borglum knew that if he was successful people would make roads to the mountain to see his work. First he worked at making clay models of the presidents' faces. Then he began working on the solid granite hundreds of feet in the air. It took him fourteen years to complete his dream, but today thousands of people have traveled to the Black Hills to see his work.

Each face Borglum carved was sixty feet long from forehead to chin. If it were possible to be so gigantic it would fit a man almost five hundred feet tall. Do you believe me? It's all right for you to believe me on this because it's the truth. But sometimes it pays to check things out for yourself. Or even better, it may pay to dream your own dreams and not just check out the dreams of others.

It doesn't cost anything to dream. And it doesn't cost anything to dream *big*. Whenever you see a Wet Paint sign I hope you'll think about the stars in the universe and the giant faces on a hillside in South Dakota. And before you touch that wet paint to test it, I hope you'll ask yourself what your own dream for the future is. What big dream are you going to make come true? Maybe you shouldn't touch the wet paint until you've decided, okay?

Sentence Prayer: Our Father, thank you for the time and the ability to dream. Amen.

ROUND AND ROUND WE GO

Prop: *A picture of a merry-go-round*

How many of you like to ride the merry-go-round when you go to an amusement park? Most children think they are lots of fun. Have you ever noticed that merry-go-rounds move in two directions. They go around and around, but at the same time they go up and down.

Riding the merry-go-round can be a lot of fun, but there's something about it that always bothers me. No matter how long a person rides, he never really gets anywhere. When he gets off his horse, he's right where he was when he started. Have you ever noticed that?

There are lots of things in life that are like the merry-go-round; they pick you up and carry you around and up and down, then let you off right where you started. Television watching, for instance. Sometimes we watch

66

TV and really learn something from watching, but many times we spend hours watching TV without reaching any worthwhile goal. The programs take us up and down and around, but they never carry us to any special goal.

Sometimes out-of-school activities can be like merry-go-rounds. They use our time; they take us up and down and around; then they let us off and we realize we haven't accomplished anything. Many times too much play activity can be a merry-go-round. We spend hours playing and at the end of the play time we're right back where we started.

Life is full of merry-go-rounds, and this isn't all bad, of course. Sometimes we need to watch TV just for fun and to join activities just for fun and to play just for the fun of it. But sometimes we get on merry-go-rounds too often or we get on by mistake, and we learn all too late that we've spent a lot of time going nowhere.

To keep this from happening, it's wise to set goals for ourselves. If your goal is to learn to play the piano, then spend some of your time practicing your piano lessons. If your goal is to own a bicycle, then spend some time working to earn money for that bike. If your goal is to make a new friend, then you'll have to spend some time being friendly to others. The people who get the most out of life are the people who set goals for themselves and spend part of their time striving to reach them. These people know where they're going, and they avoid spending too much time on merry-go-rounds that merely take them up and down and around.

Each morning why not decide how you will spend your day? Strive for a goal, then if there is time left over you'll have a chance to hunt for the merry-go-round.

Sentence Prayer: Our Father, we thank you for the ability to reach our goals. Amen.

SKY FLIERS

Prop: *Picture of a hot-air balloon*

Have you ever seen a hot-air balloon up in the sky?
The balloon may be striped with the colors of the
rainbow, and you are most likely to see it early in the
morning or just before sunset because those are the times
when the wind is usually calm.

The wind is very important to the hot-air balloonist. He
cannot steer his craft as you can steer a bicycle or a wagon.
Wind speeds and directions vary with the altitude. A
skilled balloonist can make his balloon rise and descend,
and he may be able to find air currents that will carry his
craft in the direction he wants to go. But he is always
somewhat at the mercy of the wind. He can't fly east if the
winds blow south or west, for instance.

Balloons certainly look beautiful as we see them against

a backdrop of blue sky. They look beautiful and they also look important. But as beautiful and as important as they are, do you know that they lack a feature that each one of you possesses? Can you guess what that feature is?

I'll tell you. A hot-air balloon has no brakes. The balloonist can't slow down on a whim, nor can he stop on a dime. He is at the mercy of the wind.

Now sometimes people talk as if they're filled with hot air, don't they? They just keep going and going and going and talking and talking and talking. And sometimes they say things that they really don't mean because they forgot to put the brakes on their tongues.

Do you ever do that? Do you ever say things you wish you hadn't said? We all do that sometimes, I guess. But even if this happens we know we can stop ourselves. We can put on the brakes if we want to and if we think of it in time.

Sometimes we may say things that hurt another person's feelings. Sometimes we may blurt out something that was supposed to be a secret. It's always too bad when these things happen, but there's always another time to look forward to. We can always remember that we have brakes; and we can put them on our tongues. We're not like the balloon that behaves according to the wind and the hot air inside it. We're people. We have brakes. And we have the power to use them.

Whenever you're tempted to say something you really know you shouldn't say, stop. Think about the hot-air balloon. Put on *your* brakes.

Sentence Prayer: Our Father, help us to think before we speak. Amen.

RIDDLES

Prop: *Picture of a chicken*

How many of you like riddles? I thought so. Almost everyone like a good riddle.

Riddle: Why didn't anyone want the centipede on their football team?

Answer: *It took him too long to put on his shoes.*

Riddle: What is a frightened whale called?

Answer: *Chicken of the sea.*

Riddle: Why did the farmer go over his farm with a steam roller?

Answer: *He wanted to raise mashed potatoes.*

One day a friend and I were exchanging riddles and he asked, "Why does a hen cross the road?"

Now I was really disappointed in that question. That

riddle is so old that everyone has heard it. But I answered. I said, "A hen crosses the road to see what's on the other side."

"No," my friend said. "The hen crossed the road because she heard there was a guy over there laying bricks."

I really had to laugh at that one. The answer was so much better than my answer had been. And how true to life that hen was. She wanted to go see someone who was doing something she couldn't do. We're all that way aren't we? We like to watch people who can do something we can't do.

In our minds a person who can do things we can't do becomes a hero to us—especially if we'd really like to be able to do that special thing he does.

As we go through life we must be very careful to pick heroes who do worthwhile things. And there's something else we should think about too. Did you ever realize that you could be someone else's hero? That's right. You could. If you're the fastest runner in the fourth grade, you may be a hero to some third grader who can't run nearly as fast.

Or if you're the best speller in the sixth grade, you may well be a hero to the fifth grader who missed ten words on his last spelling test. Whatever it is that you do you should remember that you may be setting an example for someone who looks up to you. If you're ever tempted to do less than your best work, just remember the riddle about the hen crossing the road to watch the man who could lay bricks.

Sentence Prayer: Our Father, we thank you for all our abilities. Help us to use them in the best ways we can. Amen.

WHO'S YOUR FAVORITE?

Prop: *A copy of* **TV Guide**

Do you have a favorite actor or actress? Maybe it's some person you see many times a week on a favorite TV program. Are you ever surprised to see that same person on some other program? TV actors and actresses play many different parts. They pretend to be many different people.

One day you may see your favorite actor playing the part of a policeman. The next day he may have the part of a doctor or a lawyer or a worker in a steel mill. Your actor has probably studied his art and craft until he can play almost any part that is assigned to him.

You may be thinking that it would be a lot of fun to be able to be lots of people instead of just the one person you are. But wait a minute! Are you just one person?

Sometimes it seems that way, but think about it carefully. I think you're probably several people. (Ask one girl to stand.)

"Now I'm going to ask you some questions. Are you a daughter?"

"Yes."

"All right. That's one person. Are you a granddaughter?"

"Yes."

"Then that makes two people that you are. Do you have an older brother or sister?"

"Yes."

"Then that makes the third person you are. You're a little sister. And do you have a younger brother or sister?"

"Yes."

"Then you are four people. You're a daughter, a granddaughter, a little sister and a big sister. Do you have some friends?"

"Yes."

"Then that's the fifth person you are." You probably didn't even guess that you were that many people, did you? But we've left out the most important person that you are. You are you.

There is nobody else on this earth who is exactly like you. If somebody wanted to pretend to be you he would have to be *acting*. So there you have it. It would take an actor to be exactly like you, but you can be you without acting at all. Someday you may want to be an actor, but for right now the very best thing to be is just yourself.

Sentence Prayer: Father, thank you for making so many different people, and thank you that I am me. Amen.

ENGLISH, ANYONE?

Prop: A *dictionary*

How many of you know what this book is? (hold up a dictionary). Right. It's a dictionary. This book is supposed to contain all the words in our language along with their definitions. As you can probably guess this is a very important book. But even so, sometimes it doesn't answer all our questions. Here's a sample of what I mean.

I heard a boy say to his grandfather. "Grandpa, I've always wanted to get on TV. Can you help me?"

Well, the grandfather thought about it for a few minutes, then he said, "Sure I can help you. First thing to do is to get your parents' permission. I don't know how you're going to do that. That's your problem. But if you get their permission, then the next thing to do is to drag a chair over to the TV set, climb onto the chair, and step over onto the TV. Be careful. And don't blame me if you fall off."

Now as you can guess, that grandfather and his grandson had a misunderstanding. The words they used with each other got twisted around in a crazy way and the grandfather really didn't understand the question. He really didn't know what his grandson wanted. So his answer was of no real value.

Does this sort of thing ever happen between you and your friends? Maybe you say a thing and your friend misinterprets it to mean something quite different from what you intended. Then what happens?

If you're not careful either you or your friend is likely to be angry. Now this is really too bad, isn't it? You meant well. Your friend meant well. But the language fouled you up. What can you do about it?

One thing that you can do whenever someone becomes angry and nobody is quite sure why is to go back over what was said. Chances are that many times you'll find that there was a simple misunderstanding. And you may find that talking the misunderstanding over will clear up the problem in hardly any time at all. It's certainly worth a try.

The next time you feel angry at a friend or the next time that you sense a friend is angry at you, why not back up and go over some of the things you've said to each other and try to find your misunderstanding. If you don't do this you may find yourself like the boy who wanted to be on TV. He knows one way to get there, but it really wasn't what he had in mind.

Sentence Prayer: Our Father, thank you for the opportunity to talk with each other and to understand each other. Amen.

DEER CROSSING

Prop: *A sign*—**Deer Crossing**

When riding along the highway how many of you have seen a sign like this one? I imagine that most of you have seen such a sign, or if you haven't seen one, you will see one if you start watching. Sometimes these signs will be seen near a timber or a river.

As a child I knew the deer couldn't read. The whole thing seemed silly. I always used to wonder why the signs were there. I never did see a deer crossing the highway at the place where the sign appeared. Then when I got a little older I learned that people really did have ways of telling where the deer crossed the highway. The deer would leave telltale signs of their passing. Sometimes you could actually see them feeding at the side of the highway or drinking from a nearby stream. Many times people could see a worn trail where deer had walked, or they could see damage the deer had done to young trees and grass and field crops.

One day when I was talking about Deer Crossing signs with my parents my dad said he was going to put up a Henry Crossing sign (using the first name of the storyteller) in our garage because he could always tell where I had been. It seems that sometimes I left my bike where it didn't belong or I forgot to replace the lawnmower in its proper spot after I used it.

Then my mother chimed in and said she was going to put up a few Henry Crossing signs in the house at spots where I left my clothes lying on the floor or my books lying on the dining room table or my model cars lying around the living room. The way she talked there might be Henry Crossing signs all over the house.

Could that happen in your house? Probably not. You all probably keep all your things in their proper places and don't cause your mother any extra work at all. But if this isn't true you might want to pause now and then and think about the Deer Crossing signs. Does your house need a sign with your name on it?

Sentence Prayer: Our Father, we thank you for our parents and our homes. Amen.

WHAT'S IN A NAME?

Prop: *A telephone directory*

Here we have a book of names. Have you ever thought about how important your name is? If it wasn't for your name people might constantly mix you up with someone else. Names are very important.

Once I knew a girl whose name was Laura Smith. Now she liked the name Laura all right, but the name Smith bothered her.

"There are so many people named Smith that it just doesn't seem very special," she said. "I looked in the telephone book and there were six pages of Smiths."

I didn't know what to tell this girl, but her grandfather did. With a twinkle in his eye he said, "Laura, Smith is a great name. Why, at one time, everyone in the world was named Smith. Didn't you know that?"

"No," Laura said. "Really?"

"Really," her grandfather said. "Everybody was named Smith. But I'll tell you what happened. Now and then some of the Smiths would do things the other Smiths didn't approve of. They might break a law or get into a fight or do some other unpleasant thing. When that happened all the other Smiths made those people change their names. Well, that went on and on, and so many people got to doing bad things that there are hardly any of us Smiths left anymore."

Laura knew her grandfather was just joking, but he had shown her that no matter what a person's name is, it is very important to that person. You take your name with you all through life. And you'll want to conduct yourself in ways that will reflect good on that name.

We all start out in life with a good name, and it's up to each of us to keep our name untarnished. The things you do reflect on your name. So whether your name is Laura Smith or John Jones the important thing is that it's *your* name and you are responsible for it.

Sentence Prayer: Our Father, we thank you for our good names. Help us to live up to them. Amen.

WHAT DO YOU WANT TO BE?

Prop: *A picture of people in different occupations*

I t's never too soon to start thinking about what you want to be when you're grown. There are so many things a person can do that it gets downright confusing. How can you decide what will be best for you?

Well, the first thing to do is to be glad that you don't have to make the decision right at the moment. You can take your time in deciding. And of course you can change your mind lots of times as you are growing up. One way to help yourself reach a decision is to learn all you can about different occupations. If you want to be a policeman, find out what a policeman has to do. When I was talking to some children one girl asked me what a person had to do to be an editor. Do you know what an editor is? An editor is a person who is in charge of putting out a paper or a magazine.

I told this child that a good editor should be able to spell and that she should know the rules of grammar. If she really wanted to be an editor she could start by doing her best in language arts at school. And since editors have to know a lot about what's going on in the world, I told this girl she could prepare herself by reading lots of books and magazines. There is hardly any occupation that doesn't require some reading.

If a certain occupation interests you, learn all you can about it. Read about it. Talk to people who are involved in it. Then ask your school teacher which things that you are studying in your classroom can help you prepare for this occupation. You may be surprised to find out how important your everyday classes may be to your future.

Sentence Prayer: Our Father, thank you for school and for teachers. Amen.

GRAB THAT BALL

Prop: *A football*

How many of you here today have thought of things that you would like to be or to do when you grow up? An astronaut? An actress? A policeman? A news reporter? A famous scientist? The list could go on and on. But when you tell others of your dream what happens?

Maybe if you tell a big brother he might say, "Oh, you can't do that, you're too little." Or someone else may say, "Oh, you can't do that, that takes a lot of hard work and talent." Or someone else may say, "Oh, you can't do that, you have to be a whiz at math." Sometimes it seems as if no matter what you say you'd like to be someone is always ready to give you lots of reasons why they think you can't do it. And if you let those people discourage you it's a sure thing that you'll fail.

So what can you do about all those people who are saying you can't? You have to look them in the eye and prove to them that you can. Now this isn't going to be an easy thing to do. But you weren't expecting it to be easy, were you?

So it's going to be hard to achieve this goal of yours. How can you manage? You might want to take a lesson from the quarterback at the football game. The quarterback faces eleven other men who are saying, "Look buddy, you can't do it. You're not big enough. You're not strong enough. You're not smart enough."

Now the quarterback could quit right then, couldn't he? But I've never seen that happen. That quarterback heads for his goal. He persuades ten other people to help him, and he does his best. Sometimes he is defeated. He has to put the ball down and start again. Sometimes he even has to give the ball to those other eleven men. But many times the quarterback does succeed in carrying the ball for a touchdown. Those are the times that are important because they prove that success is possible. Nobody will ever succeed by putting the ball down and going home. The victory goes to the person who tries until he succeeds.

The next time someone tells you you aren't big enough or smart enough or clever enough, pay no attention. Just remember the quarterback. Others will help you if you make an all-out effort to reach your goal.

Sentence Prayer: Our Father, we thank you for goals to be reached and for the power to reach them. Amen.

TOUCHDOWN

Prop: *A football helmet*

You've probably heard many times that football is a rough sport. If you've asked your parents if you could play football, you've probably heard some warning about taking safety precautions so you won't get hurt. You've probably heard a discussion of the rules of the game.

(Hold up the helmet.) You can see that this helmet will help protect a football player's head. Without it on he could get some bad bumps. And of course much more football equipment is designed to keep the player safe: shoulder pads, shin guards, special shoes. The football player goes onto the playing field prepared to face the rigors of the game.

In many ways life can be compared to a football game. It has its dangers. You can get hurt if you aren't careful.

There are rules designed to keep you safe. Look both ways before crossing the street. Don't talk to strangers. Wear your boots when it rains. You can probably think of a lot more rules than that. Some of the rules you've learned so well that you don't even have to think of them anymore. You know enough not to touch a hot stove. You probably haven't actually thought of that rule for years.

You may get tired of hearing all the rules that seem to be constantly forthcoming from teachers and parents, and maybe it will help you to have patience with all those rules if you think of them as a football suit. They're designed to help you meet the rigors of the game.

You've probably really admired the football team as it runs onto the playing field, each man in his specially designed uniform. You would think he was foolish indeed if he ran out to play ball in his ordinary street clothes. You admire the player who is prepared.

So people will admire you if you prepare yourself for the rigors of the game of life. Know the rules. Obey the rules. In everything you do in life, remember the football player. Be prepared.

Sentence Prayer: Our Father, we thank you for life and for the ability to withstand its rigors. Amen.

BLOW THE WHISTLE

Prop: *A referee's whistle*

How many of you know what this is? It's a whistle, but it's a special whistle, isn't it? It's a referee's whistle. Now you all know that the referee is the person who watches ball players to see that they are keeping all the rules of the game. When the referee sees someone break a rule, he blows his whistle, the game stops, and the player or the team may be penalized.

Players don't like to have the whistle blown on them, but they know it's the way the game is played. It makes the game fair and it makes it interesting for everyone.

You may have noticed by now that ball players aren't the only people who get the whistle blown on them. Someone is likely to blow the whistle on anyone who breaks the law. If someone drives his car too fast, a policeman may blow his whistle. If a person lets his dog run in his neighbor's yard, the neighbor may not own a whistle to blow, but he's almost sure to let the dog owner know that he has broken a law.

You people may know someone who blows the whistle on you too. Is that true? Does a playground supervisor blow a whistle if you break the rules on the playground? Does your physical education teacher blow a whistle if you break the rules of a game the class is playing?

What about around your house? Maybe your parents don't actually wear whistles, but they certainly let you know when your behavior gets out of line, don't they? You might say that they blow an imaginary whistle. And maybe you do a little whistle blowing yourself. If you have brothers or sisters, I'm guessing that you let them know if they break any of the household rules, don't you?

In a way we're very lucky to have so many people around ready to blow the whistle on us. Having people interested in our activities and in how we conduct ourselves helps us learn the proper way to do things. Sometimes we just naturally play by the rules, but other times we make mistakes and a little whistle blowing helps us learn from those mistakes. So whenever you see someone with a whistle, treat that person as a friend. You're a player in the game of life, and it's important for you to know the rules.

Sentence Prayer: Our Father, thank you for those who show us the right way to go. Amen.

HURRAH FOR MINI-GOALS!

Prop: *A miniature football goalpost*

Have you ever taken a close look at a football field? You may have been too busy looking at the ball to pay much attention to the field, but if you take a look you will notice that it is one hundred yards long and that there are goalposts like this one at each end. The fifty-yard line is right in the center of the field and every ten yards you'll see a white stripe that marks that yard line.

When a player gets the football, he knows that his ultimate goal is to carry it to the end of the field for a touchdown. But instead of thinking that he has to carry the ball fifty, sixty, or seventy yards, he probably thinks that all he really has to do is to reach the next ten-yard line. If he can reach that white stripe he has another chance to regroup, to carry the ball to the next white stripe.

We could all take a lesson from football players. We all have goals to reach and many of them seem very far off. In fact they may seem so far into the future that just thinking about all that distance makes us want to give up. Most of you people here want a highschool diploma. But if you start worrying about it today and thinking of all that work involved in earning it, you may want to give up going to school. Earning a diploma seems impossible, you may think. But it's silly to think like that.

Instead of focusing constantly on the long-range goal, a player is better advised to keep that goal in mind, but to focus his attention sharply on goals closer at hand.

You can make it through the school day tomorrow, can't you? Of course you can. And the first thing you know you'll have made it through another week, another month, then the whole school year. Goals—they are important. Sometimes the mini-goals of day-by-day living are more important than the maxi-goal at the end of the line. The mini-goals are the ones that keep people going.

When you get discouraged about whatever it is you're trying to do, remember the football field. There's a goalpost at the end of the field, but each white line marks a mini-goal on the way to a touchdown.

Sentence Prayer: Our Father, thank you for the mini-goals in our lives that encourage us along the way. Amen.

THE SEVEN WONDERS

Prop: A *picture of the Egyptian pyramids*

To the ancient Greeks and Romans there were seven wonders in the world. These wonders were: The Hanging Gardens of Babylon, the Lighthouse at Alexandria, the Colossus of Rhodes, the Mausoleum of Mausolos, the Temple of Diana at Ephesus, the statue of Olympian Zeus, and the Pyramids of Egypt. Today, except for the pyramids, all these wonders have either vanished or fallen to ruins.

This seems sad until you remember that there are many more present-day wonders all around us. Many of us won't have a chance to see wonders that are too far away, but we might like to make a list of wonders that are nearby. You might want to think about this. What would you include on your list of wonders? What wonders are right in your hometown? In your state? In your nation? Who has an idea? (Let the children talk.)

Among the wonders I would list I might include a favorite book or a piece of music or a painting. And I would want to include some wonders of nature—the volcano in Washington, for instance. And there are many wonders in the animal kingdom—birds that burrow into the earth, animals with feet that smell (no pun intended).

But even if you don't leave your own yard, your own house, your own room, you still have seven wonders right with you. Can you guess what they are?

You have your five senses. Can you name them? Each one is a wonder all in itself. Your ability to see, touch, hear, taste, and smell. Aren't those all wonders? And I can think of two more wonders. You each have the ability to think. And you each have the ability to imagine. Perhaps thinking and imagining are the greatest wonders of all.

Sentence Prayer: Our Father, we thank you for all the wonders of the world. Amen.

LOOKING BENEATH
THE SURFACE

Prop: *A can of oil*

I have a friend who comes from a long line of farm people. His grandfather owned land in Kansas and farmed it successfully for many years. His uncle inherited the farm and he too farmed it successfully for many years. Then this friend's cousin got the idea that there might be something important beneath the surface of that land. He hired men to come in with a drilling rig, and sure enough—they found oil.

For years that family had accepted the land, satisfied with its surface value. How surprised they were to find even greater riches beneath the surface.

In some ways people are like that land. People present a certain appearance to the world and the world rather accepts that appearance, satisfied that it is seeing the whole picture. From now on I hope you'll probe a little deeper in your friendships with people. Remember this farmland that was hiding oil. When you meet a person, probe beneath the surface and see what you can find.

A person whom you may see at a basketball game may be a good ballgame companion, but he could be far more. Maybe he has a secret interest in collecting stamps. Maybe he has a model train in his basement, and maybe he studies about trains and railroads. Or maybe he collects seashells and knows what sort of an animal lived in each shell.

It took time and effort for that farm family I was telling you about to discover the oil beneath the surface of their land, and it takes time and effort to discover what lies beneath the surface of the people we meet and associate with every day.

Look at your friends carefully. Enjoy the surface picture they present to the world, then probe more deeply. Let that person know you're really interested in him by inquiring into his ideas and his hobbies. And by the same token you can let him know of your specialties. Friendships are strengthened by mutual sharing. Look beneath the surface.

Sentence Prayer: Our Father, we thank you for the ability to know and to share. Amen.

LET'S KEEP BLOOMING

Prop: *A wilted flower and a fresh flower*

Almost everyone loves a bouquet of fresh flowers. Few things are lovelier than a bouquet of roses or carnations or gladiolas. In the fall months the chrysanthemum is a favorite flower with many people. But there is just one thing about cut flowers. After a few days they wilt and lose their beauty.

In Japan the people are so fond of chrysanthemum blossoms that they hold chrysanthemum festivals during the month of November. They build displays on wire frames in which pictures are formed using different colored chrysanthemum blossoms. In these beautiful and unique displays the blossoms are still attached to the plant. The chrysanthemum growers raise a special variety of plants. They use certain fertilizers that keep the plant

94

stems supple and tender enough to be bent into the display frames. These displays retain their beauty a long time because the blossoms are still attached to the plant, which is their source of strength.

In some ways people are a lot like flowers. Of course people aren't attached to any plant. They are free to move around as they please. Their source of strength is God, and as long as they are in tune with God they grow and develop in wisdom and happiness. But if they cut themselves off from God, their source of strength, then they become like a cut flower, they wither and fade.

As we travel through life we should all remember to keep the channels open to our source of strength. We can do this by attending Sunday school and church, by studying the Bible, by using thoughtful individual prayer. Let's keep blooming.

Sentence Prayer: Our Father, we thank you for your constant presence. Amen.

MOM, EVERYONE IS TEASING ME

Prop: *A picture of many children and a picture of just two or three children*

Once when I was visiting a young friend he told me that everyone was teasing him because he played with girls. So he asked me what he should do about it. Now it would be a very discouraging thing if *everyone* were teasing you about something, wouldn't it?

I questioned my friend further and I learned that *everyone* wasn't teasing him. Only a couple of the boys were teasing him. The more we talked about it the more it became evident that the ones who were doing the teasing were boys who themselves were not comfortable playing with girls. I told my friend that as he got older he would find that boys and girls played together and worked together and that nobody thought a thing about it. He decided that the best thing would be to ignore the teasers and just be himself, being a friend to anyone he really liked.

I think he made a good decision, don't you? I also think we always need to stop and consider before we jump to the conclusion that everyone is teasing us about something. It's no fun to be teased, that's for sure, and sometimes just a few people can seem like everyone. But it isn't so. If you get into a situation where you are being teased, stop and look at the situation from the point of view of the teasers.

Really, now, how many of them are there? And why do you think they're bothering to tease you? Maybe they are covering up a weakness of their own. Give them the benefit of the doubt, but while you're doing that just go right on behaving in the way that seems best for you.

Sentence Prayer: Our Father, we thank you for all people. Give us the ability to understand them and to love them. Amen.

WHAT TIME IS IT?

Prop: *A watch or two watches*

How many of you like to receive gifts? Almost everyone likes a gift, especially at Christmas time. Did you ever get two gifts that were almost the same? Sometimes this happens.

One Christmas when I was about your age I received a wristwatch from my grandparents who lived in the same town where I lived. I thought that was about the nicest gift I ever received. I wound it and set it and strapped it onto my wrist. I remember that I put it on my left wrist and all day long I pretended I was left-handed. I did things I usually did with my right hand with my left hand that day because I wanted everyone to notice my new watch. I was proud because I always knew what time it was.

Can you guess what happened? That evening my grandparents from out of town arrived for Christmas dinner. After we had eaten we settled down to open gifts and there was one for me in a big box wrapped in gold paper and tied with a red ribbon. It took me a long time to open that box. And inside it was another box. After I opened that second box I came to a third box. After a while I had opened six boxes and then I reached the last box. Can you guess what was in it? Another watch!

I was a little disappointed, but I didn't let on. I smiled, wound and set the watch, and strapped it on my right arm. But two watches presented a problem. Before I received the second watch I always knew what time it was; the watch on my left wrist told me. But then it seemed that my newest watch never showed quite the same time as the first watch did. I was never sure what time it was. One watch said one thing, and the other watch said another thing.

For a long time I was very puzzled about those watches and about what time it was. But as time passed I realized that those two watches were like two different opinions. They were never quite the same. And that's often the way it is in life. Someone asks a question, and when the answers come in you find that opinions differ. No two are the same. So you have to do just what I did with my two watches. I looked at both of them and I listened to both of them, then I decided for myself what time it was. That's about what you have to do with opinions—listen, then decide for yourself which one is the best for you.

Sentence Prayer: Our Father, we thank you for giving us the ability to see the value of opinions that differ from our own. Amen.

THE OTHER LINE
ALWAYS MOVES FASTER

Prop: A *shopping list*

Sometimes people are smart enough not to put off all their Christmas shopping until the last minute. Many times boys and girls make some of their gifts, and maybe they don't have too much shopping to do. But some shopping is usually a must. It simply has to be done.

You all know how crowded the stores are at Christmas time. People are rushing about. It's sometimes hard to walk through the aisles, and it's hard to find a clerk to wait on you. But many times the real frustration of shopping takes place when you get to the checkout line.

Have you ever noticed that no matter which line you choose to stand in to pay for your purchases, the other line always moves faster? I've noticed that. But what can you do about it?

Sometimes you can change lines. If another line looks shorter than the one you're standing in you can move to the shorter line. Have you ever done that? What happened? I don't know about you, but my own experience has been that something will happen in the shorter line that makes it start moving even more slowly than the line I just left. Maybe the cash register tape breaks and has to be replaced. Or maybe the person sacking the purchases is called away and one person has to ring up the sales as well as fill the sacks. By the time I'm outside the store I usually find that I would have been better off if I had stayed in the line I chose first.

Sometimes life can be like a shopping line. You think you see a shortcut, but it'll end up being the long way in the end. For instance when your mom tells you to clean your room, you may think you can do a speedy job by shoving everything under the bed. It's quick all right, and the room looks better at the moment.

But then what? You need something that you can't find. After you hunt for a long time, you realize that it just might be in the stuff under the bed. So out it all comes. You've spent a lot of time hunting the lost article, and guess what! Your room's a mess again. Although you hate to admit it, it would have been quicker to have cleaned the room right in the first place by putting things where they belonged.

It may seem easier to copy your homework from someone else, but later you may regret it because you didn't actually do the homework study yourself.

Whenever the task ahead of you looks long and another way looks shorter, stop. Think. The short way can take more time in the long run.

Sentence Prayer: Our Father, we thank you for giving us patience. Be patient with us as we learn to use it. Amen.

A TERRIFIC PACKAGE
OF EXPERIENCE

Prop: *A sign:* SILENCE! GENIUS AT WORK

Once there was a scientist who had invented so many useful things and written so many excellent books that people called him a genius. Now you know that a genius is a person who is very smart and very special. Well, this scientist just laughed when people called him a genius. He said: "I'm no genius. I'm just a terrific package of experience."

That statement bears thinking about. A terrific package of experience. It is said that Thomas Edison failed 10,000 times before he invented the electric light bulb. He had a terrific package of experience to guide him to his goal, didn't he?

Often we hear of someone who has just done something really great. Maybe the person has won a gold medal at the Olympics. Or maybe he has written a best-selling book. Or maybe the person has written a piece of music that we hear on the radio and TV. When this happens we are inclined to think that this person just suddenly became famous. We had never heard of him before, but now here he is with his gold medal or his best seller or his golden record. Chances are that we are seeing the end result of a terrific package of experience. The public seldom hears of the failures the famous person experienced and learned from on his way to success.

All of us are gathering experience, aren't we? We need to realize that these experiences are important to us. Every failure teaches us something. We should forget the failure and remember what we learned from it.

Never be afraid to reach out for new experiences. You may fail at them or you may succeed. But no matter which way it works out, you are stockpiling that package of experience, which is necessary for success.

Sentence Prayer: Our Father, we thank you for our successes and for our failures. Help us to learn from each. Amen.

TWENTY-FOUR HOURS

Prop: *A clock*

Everyone receives a gift at the beginning of each new day. Have you ever stopped to think about this? Are you wondering what that gift is? The gift is twenty-four hours of time. Everyone gets the same amount. The rich guy down the block doesn't get any more than the poor guy. Everyone gets the same—twenty-four hours. Since this is the case it seems to me that it is fairly important to a person's happiness and success to spend those twenty-four hours in the best way possible.

I've heard it said that work will expand to fill the time available. Have you ever thought about that? If your mother says "clean your room," and you have nothing to do that day, you can probably spend all day cleaning that room. You can make the bed, then read a chapter in a book. Then you may pick up the toys from the floor. But maybe while you're picking up you'll find a special toy and play with it awhile. First thing you know it's noon and that room still isn't cleaned up. But so what? You have the afternoon, haven't you?

But then what happens? Here comes your friend wanting to go on a hike. And you can't go because your room isn't cleaned yet. Tough. You've missed out on a good time because you didn't manage your time well.

Think how differently your day might have gone if you had known there was a hike to be taken that afternoon. You wouldn't have fooled around with cleaning your room, would you? You would have made that bed, picked up those clothes and toys, and been finished in very little time.

That's the way it goes. We each have twenty-four hours to work with, and it's up to us how we spend them. It's smart to learn to manage your day so you have time for both work and play and a little left over for just daydreaming. You're the boss. Show your time that you can manage it.

Sentence Prayer: Our Father, we thank you for each new day. Help us to get the most from it. Amen.

THE INDIVIDUAL TOUCH

Prop: *Sandwiches in different shapes*

I have a group of friends who are Girl Scouts, and I'm guessing that some of you people are Girl or Boy Scouts. Isn't that right? Well, my scouting friends were engaged in a project of making sandwiches for a picnic. Each girl had a recipe for the sandwich filling and each one worked very hard at making her sandwiches.

But when they reached the picnic and opened their boxes of sandwiches each girl was really worried. The sandwiches were all different and they hadn't counted on that. Oh, the filling was the same, but the looks were different. One girl had trimmed the crusts from her bread. Another girl had cut the bread diagonally, while others had cut theirs straight across. One girl had even used a cookie cutter on the bread and made round sandwiches.

But the scout leader didn't care that the sandwiches didn't look alike. And at the picnic nobody cared. They liked every sandwich, finding one just as good as another.

People are a lot like those sandwiches. They may differ a lot in their looks and their actions, but in their inner feelings they differ hardly at all. Every person knows and understands happiness and hurt. In that way people are all alike, and it's the inner part of a person that's really the important part, isn't it?

Whenever you see people who look different to you, remember those Girl Scout sandwiches. Outer differences really don't matter; it's what's inside that really counts.

Sentence Prayer: Our Father, we thank you for our similarities as well as for our differences. Amen.

WATCH THE BRIDGES

Prop: *A picture of a bridge*

When you live in a place where it gets very cold in the winter you learn to take certain precautions. Now I grew up where we had lots of snow and ice in the winter and I can remember a warning my mother frequently called out to my father as he left for work in the mornings. She would say: "Be careful, Bill. You know it may be slick on the bridges. Watch the bridges."

Now that was good advice. The roads and highways could be perfectly dry, but on the bridges there was likely to be a glaze of ice that could send a car into a spin. My father drove for many years without an accident, and I've always thought that he owed part of that success to being careful on the bridges. When a person knows where the danger spots are, he should try to avoid them.

Everyone likes to have a lot of friends, but in some ways friends are a lot like bridges. Many times they'll have danger spots. If you want to keep your friendships in good repair you'll avoid those danger spots, or at least approach them with caution. If you know that Mary is sensitive about being a poor reader, you'll be smart not to point that fact out to her if you value her friendship. If you know that Bill hates being so short, you'll do nothing to call that fact to his attention. Most people have certain things that they feel sensitive about. You probably have some yourself, don't you?

In dealing with other people whom you want to be your friends, always be aware of the danger areas. In this life you'll have a better chance of getting along with people if you'll just remember that it might be slick on the bridges.

Sentence Prayer: Our Father, thank you for our friends. Help us to be kind to them. Amen.

PROMISES
AND TURTLE SHELLS

Prop: *A turtle's shell or a picture showing a turtle's shell*

C hildren in Trinidad often hear a folktale that tells why a turtle's shell looks cracked. According to this tale there was a turtle named Martin who had two problems: he was always hungry, and he wished he could fly like his friends the birds. No matter how hard he tried he just couldn't get enough to eat nor could he get off the ground.

Then one day Mr. Hawk invited all the birds to a party on a faraway mountaintop. Martin the Turtle felt very sad because he wasn't invited. When the other birds saw how sad he felt they each donated a feather to him. Martin tucked all the feathers under his shell, and sure enough—he could fly.

The next day Martin and the birds flew to Mr. Hawk's

party. Right away Mr. Hawk noticed that Martin didn't look like the rest of the birds, but he welcomed him when the other guests claimed Martin as their friend.

As usual Martin was hungry. When he saw the wonderful refreshments Mr. Hawk had prepared for the party his mouth watered. Martin began grabbing and eating all the tidbits in sight: pigeon peas, avacados, mangoes. He thought he had never had it so good. He didn't notice that all the other guests were staring at him. And Mr. Hawk was really glaring at him.

At last the birds grew very disgusted with Martin because he was showing such bad manners. They flew at him, pecked him, and forced him from the refreshment table. Then they chased him until he lost his balance and rolled down the mountainside. His feathers didn't help him. He could no longer fly.

When Martin reached the foot of the mountain, his shell was badly scratched and cracked. He patched it as well as he could, but even after the shell healed, traces of the cracks could be seen. In fact, if you could find Martin today you still could see those cracks in his shell.

You may be able to think of several things that are a lot like a turtle shell—that is, once broken they can be mended, but they are never quite the same again. Sometimes toys are broken and mended. Or dishes. Or promises. But these things are never quite right after that, are they?

Let's think about promises. If a promise is broken, how do you feel about the person who didn't keep his word? You never feel quite the same about that person, do you?

Sometimes promises are very hard to keep. It's wise to think for a long time before making a promise, and if you're ever tempted to go back on your word and break a promise, just think about the story of Martin the Turtle and his cracked shell. Nothing is ever quite the same once it has been broken.

Sentence prayer: Our Father, help us to keep our promises to each other. Amen.